102
Br

Tornadoes

Tornadoes

Peter Murray

THE CHILD'S WORLD, INC.

Library of Congress Cataloging-in-Publication Data
Murray, Peter, 1952 Sept. 29–
Tornadoes / by Peter Murray.
p.   cm.
Includes index.
Summary: Describes tornadoes, how they form,
their destructive capabilities, and safety
precautions that people should know.
ISBN 1-56766-548-9 (alk. paper)
1. Tornadoes—Juvenile literature.
[1. Tornadoes.]   I. Title.
QC955.2.M87   1998
551.55'3—dc21   98-6138
CIP
AC

Photo Credits

© Beryl Bidwell/Tony Stone Images: 9
© Charles Doswell III/Tony Stone Images: 15, 24
© G. Brad Lewis/Tony Stone Images: 2
© 1991 H. Stein/Weatherstock: 30
© 1991 Keith Brewster/Weatherstock: 16
© 1982 J. Leonard/Weatherstock: 26
© 1997 Mark A. Schneider/Dembinsky Photo Assoc. Inc: 23
©1989 R. Britt/Weatherstock: cover
© Sheila Beougher/Liason International: 13
© Warren Faidley/Weatherstock: 29
© 1989 Warren Faidley/Weatherstock: 6
© 1991 Warren Faidley/Weatherstock: 19
© 1993 Weatherstock/NOAA: 20
© 1994 Warren Faidley/Weatherstock: 10

On the cover...

Front cover: This Texas tornado is turning black as it picks up dirt.
Page 2: Tornadoes like this one can be very dangerous.

Table of Contents

It is late in the afternoon on a hot summer day. The air is still and thick and moist. Tall, fluffy clouds appear in the sky. As they move toward you, you can see their dark undersides.

Over a few hours, the air cools and the sky takes on a strange, yellowish glow. A wind begins to blow, getting stronger every minute. Soon it whips your hair against your cheeks. A scrap of paper goes sailing up into the air. Tree branches bend, weeds tumble across the grass, and leaves fly through the air. Maybe it's time to take shelter! This could be tornado weather.

Dark storm clouds like this one sometimes bring tornadoes. ⇒

From the safety of your house, you watch the dark clouds. You see rain falling and a flash of lightning. Seconds later, you hear crackling thunder. The underside of the thundercloud bulges and twists around itself. The bulge begins to spin faster and faster. Soon a cone-like shape drops from the cloud. This shape is called a **funnel cloud**.

⇐ This funnel cloud is forming during a storm in Arizona.

As the funnel cloud stretches downward, you hear a rushing sound. The tip of the funnel waves and dances above the ground. For a moment, it looks as though it will return to the clouds.

Suddenly the tip drops down, touching the ground. A dark cloud boils up from the spinning cone. Dirt and dust are sucked into it, instantly turning the cone dark gray. You hear a sound like a freight train, getting louder, coming right at you. The funnel cloud has become a tornado!

This huge tornado is picking up a lot of dirt. ⇒

How Long Do Tornadoes Last?

Some tornadoes last only a few seconds. Others last for hours. Tornadoes can spin in one place or travel faster than a car. When you see a tornado coming, there is only one smart thing to do—take shelter!

This Texas tornado is moving quickly towards a small town. ⇒

Where Do Most Tornadoes Happen?

Hundreds of tornadoes touch down in North America's "Tornado Alley" every year. Tornado Alley includes most of the central United States, from Texas to Minnesota. In those areas, warm, moist air from the Gulf of Mexico meets cool, dry air from Canada. The air swirls around itself, creating powerful winds.

As the moist air rises high into the air, it packs tightly together, or **condenses**. The winds and moist air keep moving, forming towering thunderclouds. This is the perfect weather for thunderstorms. And wherever there are thunderstorms, tornadoes are possible.

These storm clouds are full of moist air. ⇒

Tornadoes are most likely to happen in North America or Australia. But that doesn't mean they don't happen in other areas. In fact, tornadoes happen even in the middle of the ocean! When tornadoes form over water, they are called **waterspouts**.

⇐ This waterspout is picking up water near the Florida coast.

Do Tornadoes Cause Damage?

Most tornadoes do little damage. They touch down in open areas such as fields. They last only a few minutes, and then they disappear.

Other tornadoes are not so friendly. In 1965, six states were hit by a series of 37 tornadoes. The tornadoes caused 271 deaths. The worst tornado on record was the famous *Tri-State Tornado* of 1925. This giant tornado traveled 219 miles through Missouri, Illinois, and Indiana. It killed 689 people and ruined 1,100 homes.

A tornado did a lot of damage in this Kentucky neighborhood. ⇒

How Do Tornadoes Destroy Things?

Tornadoes produce the most powerful winds on Earth. In fact, a large tornado can create winds of up to 300 miles per hour. That's strong enough to blow a railroad car off its track!

Tornadoes are also dangerous because of their spinning. A tornado's swirling winds create a **vacuum** inside the funnel. The vacuum can suck things in or blow them apart. When the funnel passes over a house, the vacuum and the winds can cause the house to explode. Sometimes the tornado's vacuum sucks up cars, trees, and even people.

⇐ This tornado just caused some damage in an Oklahoma town.

How Can We Stay Safe During Tornadoes?

Even if you live right in the middle of Tornado Alley, you might never see a twister. Only about one thunderstorm out of a thousand produces a tornado. Still, it's smart to be prepared. Knowing what to do in a tornado can save your life.

← This tornado in Texas is very near to a farmhouse.

Never try to outrun a tornado in a car or on your bike. Even though they might look slow, tornadoes are very fast and can change directions quickly. And don't stay outside to watch it! The safest place to be during a tornado is inside.

At the first sign of a tornado, you should head for your house. If you have a basement or a storm cellar, that's where you should be. If you don't have a basement, hide in a closet or under a heavy table. And stay away from windows! Most people injured in tornadoes are hurt by falling objects or broken glass.

Tornadoes like this Arizona twister can be very dangerous. ⇒

Today, scientists are trying to learn as much as they can about tornadoes. They study the winds and clouds of thunderstorms before tornadoes form. They also try to predict where each tornado will touch down. By learning more about tornadoes, scientists may one day be able to keep people safe from these powerful forces of nature.

Glossary

condenses (kon–DEN–sez)
When something condenses, it becomes tightly packed together. Moist air condenses in clouds to form rain and snow.

funnel cloud (FUH–null KLOWD)
A funnel cloud is a cone-shaped cloud in a storm. Many funnel clouds turn into tornadoes.

waterspout (WAH–ter–spowt))
A water spout is a tornado that forms over water.

vacuum (VAK–yoom)
A vacuum can suck things in or blow them apart. Swirling winds inside a tornado's funnel create a vacuum.

Index